French Chic

DECORATIVE HOME EMBROIDERY

100 IDEES
Ballantine Books · New York

Conceived, designed and produced by
Conran Octopus Limited
28-32 Shelton Street
London WC2 9PH

Editor: Diana Mansour
Contributing Editor: Jan Eaton
Art Editor: Caroline Murray
Illustrators: Paul Cooper, Coral Mula,
Prue Bucknell

Library of Congress Catalog Card Number 86-92110

ISBN 345-34718-8

Manufactured in Hong Kong

First American Edition: August 1987

10 9 8 7 6 5 4 3 2 1

Acknowledgments (Photographer/Stylist)

1 G. de Chabaneix/C. de Chabaneix
4-5 G. Bouchet/C. Lebeau
8-13 M. Duffas/I. Garçon
14-16 M. Duffas/J. Schoumacher
18-19 J. Dirand/C. Lebeau
23-24 M. Duffas/I. Garçon
26-29 B. Maltaverne/C. Lebeau
30-35 J. Dirand/C. Lebeau
36-38 M. Duffas/I. Garçon
40-44 G. De Chabaneix/I. Garçon
46-49 M. Duffas/J. Schoumacher
51-53 M. Duffas/J. Schoumacher/I. Garçon
54-56 G. Bouchet/C. Lebeau
58 N. Bruant/C. Lebeau
59 C. Lebeau/C. Lebeau
63 J. Dirand/C. Lebeau
64-66 V. Assenat/J. Schoumacher
68-71 G. Bouchet/C. de Chabaneix
72-74 G. de Chabaneix/C. de Chabaneix
76-78 J. Dirand/C. Lebeau

CONTENTS

INTRODUCTION

It is very satisfying to look around your home and see touches of hand embroidery here and there – a set of cushion covers perhaps, or a pretty tablecloth – but even more rewarding if, when your friends compliment you on these unique and elegant items, you can modestly reply that you made them yourself. This book is filled with a host of delightful and unusual embroidery designs for home furnishings and linens, all with a touch of French flair and charm, for people of all levels of skill.

There is a wide range of embroidery types to choose from, including needlepoint (shopping bags, a flower-patterned chair cover, a rug and a teacosy), satin and other surface stitches (tablecloths, cushion covers and bed linen), shadow work, and even a project which includes some decorative machine stitching (see page 8). Some of the designs, such as the Ming vase cushions on page 76, are complex, not so much because of the stitches used as because of the intricacy of the pattern and the large number of colors which must be skilfully blended to achieve the effect of blue-and-white vases overflowing with beautiful flowers. These designs will prove an irresistable and interesting challenge to the more experienced embroideress. Other projects, such as the adorable Easter tablecloth – a typical expression of the French love for and enjoyment of children – are smaller in scale and easier to work.

Embroideries, because they take time and care to make, are generally stitched on good quality fabrics, using long lasting threads, so that you can continue to enjoy them for years. Many of the items in this book, like the very elegant pink damask tablecloth on page 64, with its sprays of flowers and grasses, could well become treasured family heirlooms, carefully looked after and passed down to future generations.

Although the designs in this book are all used for specific items, most could be used for other purposes: the leaves, insects and fruits on page 68 would look equally as charming on a roller blind as on a tablecloth, the design on the Hungarian duvet cover on page 40 was taken from folk costume and could easily be used on clothing, or the simple motifs on the fish apron on page 50 could be used to make a highly individual set of napkins to amuse seafood addicts; for as well as offering great artistic pleasure, embroidery is fun.

BASIC ESSENTIALS

Most of the designs in this book are shown smaller than actual size. The method used to enlarge them is perfectly straightforward and is explained below, as are the standard embroidery techniques and stitches required. Specific skills relating to particular projects are described within the main text.

ENLARGING A DESIGN

Enlarging the designs in this book to the correct size is not difficult to do successfully, but accurate measuring is important. Basically, the technique consists of dividing the original design into equal squares and then carefully copying the design, square for square, onto a larger grid. First trace the design from the book onto a piece of tracing paper, centering it and following the diagrams shown on this page. The most accurate way to copy the image is to mark each place where the design lines cross the larger grid, and then join up these marks.

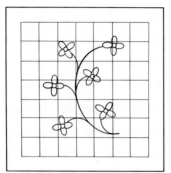

drawn from the smaller grid.

Copy the design, square for square, onto the large-scale grid, then check it against the original.

TRANSFERRING A DESIGN

When the design has been enlarged to the correct size, you will need to transfer it onto the fabric before the embroidery is begun. Carbon paper works well on most fabrics and is quick and easy. Use dressmakers' carbon paper, which is available in different colors, rather than the type sold by a stationer.

Using masking tape at the corners to hold it firm, place the fabric over a flat surface. Tape the design tracing over the fabric, then slip the carbon paper face down between the fabric and the tracing and trace over the outlines.

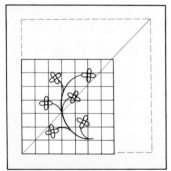

Draw a grid square over the tracing and draw in a diagonal. Using this line as a guide, mark the outline of the full-size square or rectangle on a larger piece of tracing paper. Next draw a grid of the same number of squares, but larger in size, as on the small trace.

For example, if there is already a grid shown in the book and each square represents a square of 2in (5cm), draw the large-scale grid to these dimensions. If the design has no grid but is, say, half size, then draw a squared grid on tracing paper and tape it over the design. Trace the design then draw up a large grid, doubling the size and making sure that the top right corner meets a diagonal

EMBROIDERY FRAMES

All embroidery will be more successful if the fabric or canvas is held taut in an embroidery frame. It is not only easier to handle, but the stitches will be more regular and distortion of the fabric kept to a minimum. There are several types of frame available, and the choice depends on the fabric, the size of the project and your own preference. A simple round frame or hoop is suitable for embroidery on plain-weave fabrics. If the project is quite large, the hoop can be quickly and easily moved along the fabric after a portion of the stitching has been completed. Canvas should be stretched in a rectangular frame large enough to accommodate the whole piece. The simplest rectangular frame is a wooden stretcher to which the canvas is attached by drawing pins or staples. You can make a stretcher from four wooden battens joined at the corners, or they are available in a wide range. Specialist embroidery frames are adjustable and stretch the fabric very evenly. A hoop or a rectangular frame can be used with even-weave fabric.

PRESSING

Embroidery on fabric will need a light pressing to smooth out any wrinkles in the fabric caused by the stitching.

Before pressing, pad the ironing board with a thick folded towel and lay the embroidery over it, face down.

Cover the embroidery with a damp piece of thin cotton fabric and press lightly, letting the iron just touch the pressing cloth. Take care not to crush heavily stitched areas. Let the embroidery dry thoroughly.

BLOCKING

Canvaswork should be blocked to straighten the canvas, which becomes distorted during the stitching, even in an embroidery frame. For blocking, you will need a piece of wood or blockboard larger than the embroidery and covered with a sheet of clean polythene; rustproof tacks; a hammer; a steel rule or tape measure; a water spray or sponge.

If the canvas has a selvage, cut small nicks along it to ensure that it stretches evenly.

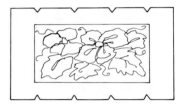

Damp the canvaswork with the spray or a wet sponge and place it face down on the board. Lightly hammer tacks at center top and bottom of the surplus canvas, stretching the canvas gently downwards. Repeat this at each side, checking that the warp and weft threads of the canvas are at right angles to each other.

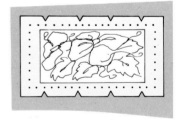

Working outwards from the center of each side, insert more tacks at ¾in (2cm) intervals, stretching the canvas gently as you proceed.

Check the size and shape of the canvas to make sure the stretching is even. Adjust the tacks where necessary. Hammer all the tacks in securely. Spray or sponge the canvas all over and let it dry at room temperature for several days. A second blocking may be needed to straighten strongly vertical or horizontal designs.

MITERING CORNERS ON CANVAS

This way of finishing corners on canvaswork will give a neat edge without bulk. Always block the canvas before finishing the edges.

Trim the corner of the surplus canvas to reduce the bulk.

Turn over the canvas to the corner of the embroidery.

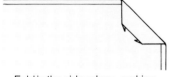

Fold in the side edges, making sure that the corner is square, and tack in place. Secure the edge and the mitered corner with a row of hand stitching.

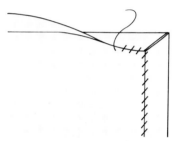

MITERING CORNERS ON FABRIC

This method of finishing corners on a piece of fabric will ensure a neat, crisp finish.

Fold over a narrow hem along each edge of the fabric and press. Trim the corner to reduce bulk, turn over the corner and press.

Fold over the two sides as shown and pin in place. Hand or machine stitch along the hem. Hand stitch the diagonal joining if the hem is quite wide.

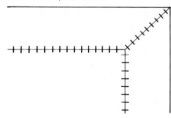

Note Some of the stitches used in this book have been shown with specific projects: for *cross stitch* see page 36, *antique hem stitch* (drawn-thread) see page 62, *stem stitch* and *long and short stitch* see page 68, *closed herringbone stitch* see page 72 and *chain stitch* see page 76.

EMBROIDERY STITCHES

The stitches used on the projects are shown below, and they are all quite simple to work. With some of the stitches such as satin stitch and long and short stitch, practice will be needed to work them neatly and get good fabric coverage. Follow the diagrams carefully if the stitch is one you are not familiar with.

Work with the fabric or canvas stretched in an embroidery hoop or frame as this will help you to keep the stitches regular. Remember not to pull the threads too tightly. The individual instructions will give you details of how to work the designs, where to start stitching, how many strands of thread to use, and suggested needle sizes.

Do not use a knot on the back of the fabric or canvas. It produces an unsightly bulge on the right side. Instead, leave a short tail of thread hanging, use the needleful of thread and then secure the ends through the stitches on the wrong side.

straight stitch

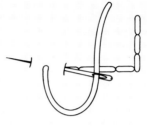

back stitch

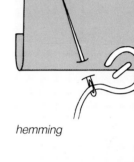

hemming

satin stitch

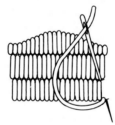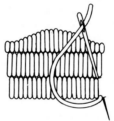

encroaching satin stitch

Chinese knots

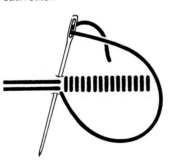

couching

seed stitch

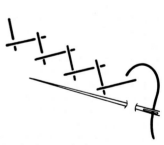

herringbone stitch

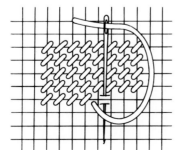

half cross stitch

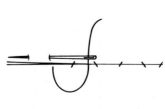

slip stitch

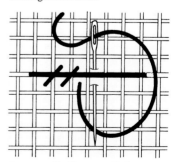

trammed half cross stitch

DRAGONFLY BEDLINEN

There is no need to lie awake counting sheep when you could sleep peacefully, dreaming of dragonflies dancing over water. This very delicate set consists of a pillowcase hand embroidered with dragonfly motifs and a machine embroidered and quilted duvet cover, crossed and edged with silver piping, and a pillowcase to match. The cover is of a typically French design, with the center left open so that the duvet can be inserted through it. If you prefer, you could fill the central square and make a conventional opening at the bottom (see page 42).

Sizes Finished duvet cover 80in × 80in (200cm × 200cm) to fit standard double duvet; pillowcases 30in × 22in (75cm × 55cm).

MATERIALS

DRAGONFLY PILLOWCASE
1 ½yd (1.4m) of 36in (90cm) wide white cotton piqué
3yd (2.7m) of ready-made (washable) silver piping
White sewing thread
Crewel needle size 4 or 5
Dressmakers' carbon paper
Large embroidery hoop

GEOMETRIC PILLOWCASE
1 ½yd (1.4m) of 36in (90cm) wide white cotton piqué
5½yd (5m) of ready-made
(washable) silver piping
White sewing thread

DUVET COVER
5¾yd (5.2m) of 36in (90cm) wide white cotton piqué
4¾yd (4.2m) of 88in (220cm) wide cotton sheeting for back and inner lining
2yd (2m) of 100in (250cm) wide
medium-weight polyester wadding
30½yd (28m) of ready-made (washable) silver piping
White sewing thread
Light colored pencil

Threads
DRAGONFLY PILLOWCASE
Two reels of DMC **silver** thread 281
Anchor coton à broder size 16:
one skein each of **gray** 398 and 399, and two skeins of **white** 1

GEOMETRIC PILLOWCASE
Two reels of DMC **silver** thread 281

Embroidery stitches
Couching, padded satin stitch; these are used in the Dragonfly pillowcase. The Geometric pillowcase and the Duvet cover are both machine stitched.

DIRECTIONS

DRAGONFLY PILLOWCASE
▦ Cut a piece measuring 32in × 32in (80cm × 60cm) from the fabric. This will be the front of the pillowcase.
▦ Trace the dragonfly design and enlarge it to the required dimensions, as shown on page 6.

▦ Using the photograph as a guide to position, transfer the design to the top left-hand corner of the fabric, using dressmakers' carbon paper and leaving a margin of 1in (2.5cm) from the raw edges.
▦ Working with the fabric stretched in the embroidery hoop, embroider the lines in couched silver thread and the dragonflies in padded satin stitch with the white thread. Embroider the spots in padded satin stitch in a random mixture of silver, white and gray, as seen in the photograph.
▦ When you have finished the embroidery, place the fabric face down on a well-padded surface and press it lightly, taking care not to crush the stitches. Trim the edges so that the finished front section measures 31¼in × 23¼in (78cm × 58cm).

FINISHING THE PILLOWCASE
▦ Cut out a rectangle of fabric 32⅝in × 23¼in (81.5cm × 58cm) for the back and another rectangle 23¼in × 7in (58cm × 17.5cm) for the flap.
▦ Turn under 2in (5cm) to the wrong side along one short edge of the back piece and then turn under ⅜in (1cm) along the raw edge to make a 1⅝in (2in) deep hem. Stitch in place.
▦ Turn under a double 2in (5cm) hem to the wrong side along one long edge of the flap. Pin, tack and stitch in place.
▦ Pin the piping to the right side of the embroidered front. The piping should face inwards to the center all around the edge. Stitch the piping in place ⅝in (1.5cm) from the raw edges.
▦ Assemble the pillowcase by placing the back section on top of the piped front with the right sides of the fabric facing. Align the hemmed edge of the back with the seam line on the front. Place the flap right side down over the hemmed edge of the back, matching the long raw edge of the flap with the raw edge on the front. Pin, tack and stitch, following the line of stitching for the piping.
▦ Trim and finish the raw edges, then turn the pillowcase right side out with the flap on the inside. Press the seams.

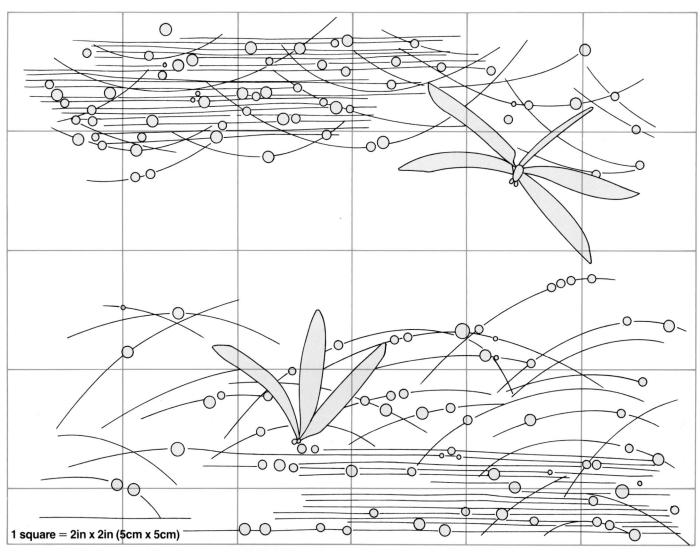

1 square = 2in x 2in (5cm x 5cm)

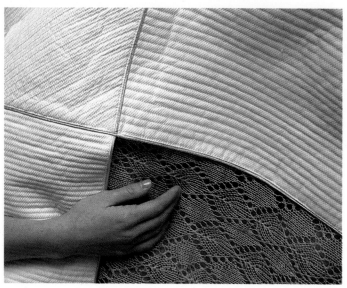

GEOMETRIC PILLOWCASE

▦ Cut a piece of cotton piqué to measure 25½cm × 17¼in (63cm × 43cm) for the center front.

▦ With silver thread on top and white sewing cotton in the bobbin, stitch the pattern of crossing lines. Use the photograph as a guide, and position the outermost lines 5in (12.5cm) from the raw edges of the fabric.

▦ Pin the piping to the right side of the fabric. It should face towards the center and run all around the edge. Stitch the piping in place ⅝in (1.5cm) from the raw edges.

▦ Cut two strips of fabric measuring 23¼cm × 4¼in (58cm × 10.5cm) and two strips measuring 31¼in × 4¼in (78cm × 10.5cm). Join the strips into a

frame with mitered darts, starting ⅝in (1.5cm) away from the raw inner edge and tapering to nothing at the outside edge. Trim and press.

▦ Stitch the border frame to the central piece, following the stitching line of the piping and stitching the two long sides first and then the two short ones.

▦ Finish the pillowcase in the same way as the dragonfly pillowcase.

DUVET COVER

▦ Cut eight rectangles measuring 25¼in × 25¼in (63cm × 63cm) and cut the same from wadding.

▦ Using light colored pencil, draw the seam line on the right side around each fabric piece, ⅝in

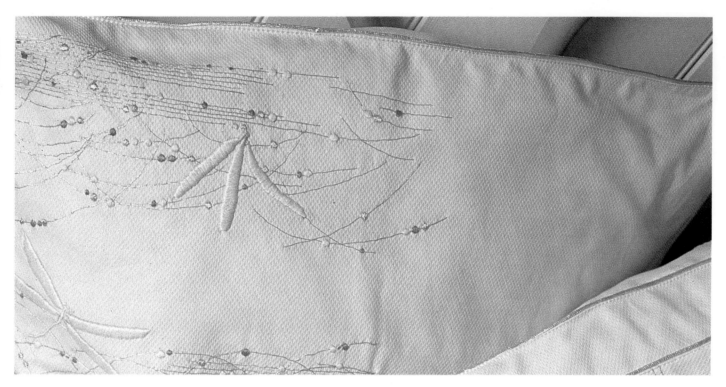

(1.5cm) from the raw edge.

▦ Back each fabric piece with a piece of wadding and tack horizontally and vertically. Using the diagram as a guide, quilt each of the squares with long machine straight stitches and the white sewing thread.

▦ Cut 25¼in (63cm) lengths of piping and stitch one each to the bottom edges of A, B and C and the top edges of F, G and H.

▦ Stitch A, D and F together to make a long strip. Trim wadding back to the seam line and trim ⅜in and ¼in (1cm and 5mm) from the seam allowances of the piping cord at each side of the seams, to layer the seam allowances. Press seams open.

▦ Join C, E and H in the same way. Stitch a length of piping, with the piping lying inwards and raw edges matching, to the inside edge of each long strip.

▦ Following the diagram, join rectangles B and G to the strips to complete the patchwork effect. Topstitch along all seams, except around the center, close to piping.

▦ Pin piping around the outer edge, rounding the corners gently and with the piping facing inwards. Stitch in position.

▦ Cut four strips of piqué and four of wadding, each measuring 81¼in × 7in (203cm × 17.5cm). Pin and tack wadding to the back of each strip, then join the strips, as for the Geometric pillowcase, to make a mitered border frame.

▦ Turn under the seam allowance around the quilted piece and topstitch it to the border, stitching just inside the piping.

▦ Cut two pieces of cotton sheeting the same size as the top. Set one piece aside and pin and stitch the other piece to the top, with right sides together and stitching around the edge of the central opening, following the seam lines of the piping. Cut out the central square from the sheeting and take to the back.

▦ Topstitch around the central opening, close to the piping.

▦ Pin piping around the outer edge, pinning through the top and the backing, with raw edges matching. Stitch in position.

▦ With right sides of duvet top and second piece of sheeting together, stitch around the outer edge, following the line of the piping, and leaving a gap for turning. Turn to the right side and slipstitch to close.

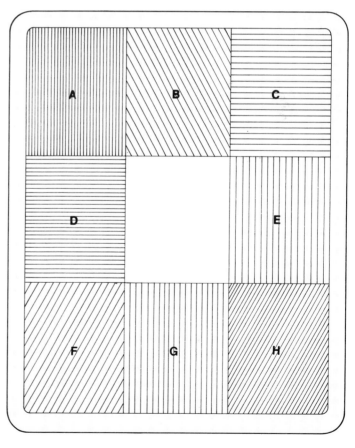

CRAZY CROSS STITCH

A far cry from the conventional flower-patterned needlepoint, this unusual cross-stitch design features a bold, humorous medley of letters, symbols and colors, with elements of both 1930s and 1950s decorative styles. The result is a colorful rug that will harmonize with most modern settings. If you want to add a personal touch, you could easily substitute your initials for some of the letters, keeping to the same large block capitals with drawing pin circles at the joins.

Size Approximately 63½in × 55in (159cm × 138cm).

MATERIALS

2yd × 1¾yd (1.8m × 1.6m) of 4-gauge rug canvas	Large tapestry or rug needle
Strong sewing thread	Fine-tip waterproof felt marker
	Wide masking tape

Threads
*Pingouin rug yarn (if this is not available, substitute the same colors from another range): 16 balls of **gray** 30; nine balls of **black** 36; four balls each of **red** 43, **yellow** 61 and **orange** 52; three balls each of **bright** **blue** 60, **pink** 51 and **white** 05; two balls each of **turquoise** 55, **sky blue** 65, **jade green** 71, **green** 58 and **rose pink** 15; one ball each of **brown** 08, **French blue** 34 and **brick** 14*

Embroidery stitches
Cross stitch worked in two journeys (see below); each square on the chart represents one cross stitch.
Herringbone stitch for finishing the edges.

DIRECTIONS

▦ Draw a vertical line with the waterproof marker down the center of the canvas, taking care not to cross any vertical threads. Mark the central horizontal line in the same way. Rule corresponding lines across the chart to find the center of the design.

▦ Bind the edges of the canvas with masking tape to prevent the threads unravelling. Begin stitching at the center of the canvas, working outwards from the center of the design and following the chart square by square. To make the canvas easier to handle, roll up those areas on which you are not working.

▦ Make each horizontal line of cross stitch in two journeys. Stitch the left to right diagonals on the first journey and complete the crosses on the second journey by filling in the right to left diagonals.

▦ When all the stitching has been completed, block the embroidery (see page 6) if it has pulled out of shape. Trim the surplus canvas away leaving a margin of 4in (10cm) of unworked canvas all around the embroidery.

▦ On the reverse of the rug, turn in the margin (see page 7 for instructions on mitering corners) and secure the edges with a row of herringbone stitch in strong thread.

▦ Alternatively, use strips of carpet webbing, overlapping them at the corners. Backstitch the strips to the rug, then miter and stitch them as shown.

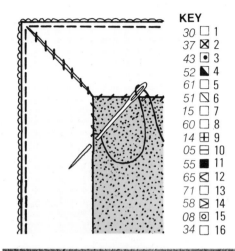

KEY

30	☐	1
37	☒	2
43	⊡	3
52	◼	4
61	☐	5
51	◨	6
15	☐	7
60	☐	8
14	⊞	9
05	☐	10
55	◼	11
65	◩	12
71	◪	13
58	◧	14
08	⊙	15
34	☐	16

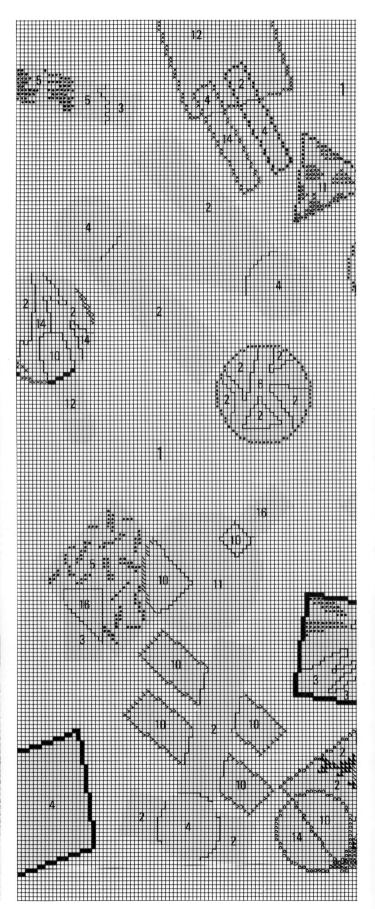

TULIP TIME

Use it as a wall hanging, an unusual table runner or even as a mat: whichever you choose, this bright needlepoint picture with its vivid, life-size tulips and anemones will catch the eye and lift the spirits. The zingy reds and pinks, glowing all the more against the green contrast of the leaves, blend happily with the clean, simple lines of modern furnishings.

Size Approximately 80in × 24in (200cm × 60cm).

MATERIALS

2½yd × 28in (2.2m × 70cm) of double-thread 12-gauge canvas
2½yd (2.2m) of 36in (90cm) wide cotton fabric in a neutral color, for the lining
Matching strong sewing thread
Tapestry needle size 18 or 20
Fine-tip waterproof felt marker

Medium-tip black felt marker
Rotating embroidery frame, large enough to accommodate the width of the canvas
Wide masking tape
82in (205cm) strip of 4in (10cm) wide webbing, optional, for a casing if the panel is to be hung

Threads

DMC tapestry yarn: one skein each of **green** 7342, 7370, 7604 and 7912, **pink** 7153, **yellow** 7784 and 7973, and **mauve** 7247; two skeins each of **blue** 7797, **green** 7345, 7386 and 7540, **ecru, pink** 7103, 7106, 7135 and 7151, **red** 7137, **yellow** 7726, and **mauve** 7245; three skeins each of **green** 7596 and 7988, **pink** 7136, and **mauve** 7243; four skeins of **green** 7344; five skeins each of **red** 7640; six skeins each of **black**, and **green** 7861; seven skeins each of **red** 7606 and 7666; eight skeins of **pink** 7157; nine skeins each of **green** 7943 and 7547, and **pink** 7155; 17 skeins each of **blue** 7820 and 7995, and 29 skeins of **beige** 7280

Embroidery stitches

Trammed half cross stitch for the plain background, flowers and pots; half cross stitch for the checkerboard background, and herringbone stitch for finishing the edges.

1

DIRECTIONS

THE EMBROIDERY

▦ Trace the design and then enlarge it to the dimensions given. Strengthen the design lines with the felt marker.

▦ Place the canvas over the design, leaving a 4in (10cm) margin of surplus canvas around all the edges. The design lines will now be visible through the canvas. Using the waterproof felt marker, trace the design carefully onto the canvas.

▦ Bind the two long edges of the canvas with masking tape to prevent them fraying and then mount the canvas in the rotating embroidery frame.

▦ Starting at one edge and working each area of color separately, embroider the checkerboard background in half cross stitch and the rest of the design in trammed half cross stitch.

▦ When all the embroidery has been completed, remove the embroidery frame.

▦ Block the embroidery (see page 6) if it has pulled out of shape, paying special attention to the checkerboard pattern, in which the squares should be regular.

FINISHING THE PANEL

▦ Leaving a margin of 2in (5cm) all around the embroidered area, trim away the surplus canvas.

Mitering the corners, turn the unworked edges to the back and secure them with herringbone stitch.

To make the lining, cut a rectangle of lining fabric 1in (2.5cm) larger than the finished embroidery on all edges. Turn in and press a generous 1in (2.5cm) single hem all around, making sure that the finished size of the lining is slightly smaller than the embroidery.

If you wish to hang the picture, turn in the short ends of the webbing by 1in (2.5cm). Position the webbing ¾in (2cm) below top edge of lining and machine stitch along the top edge. Lay the lining on a flat surface; take the hanging pole and fold the webbing over it. Pin along the bottom edge of the webbing; remove the pole, and then stitch along the pinned edge.

Fold the lining vertically in half, bringing right sides together. Using locking stitch, in which the thread is taken alternately through the back of the embroidery and then through the lining, join the lining to the back of the finished embroidery down the center. Working first out to one side then out to the other, join the lining to the back of the embroidery with additional vertical lines of stitching approximately 10in (25cm) apart, always taking care not to stitch through the webbing sleeve. Finish by slipstitching around all edges.

KEY

a 7342	**j** 7345	**t** 7245	**D** 7606
b 7370	**k** 7386	**u** 7596	**E** 7666
c 7604	**l** 7540	**v** 7988	**F** 7157
d 7912	**m** *ecru*	**w** 7136	**G** 7943
e 7153	**n** 7103	**x** 7243	**H** 7155
f 7784	**o** 7106	**y** 7344	**I** 7820
g 7973	**p** 7135	**z** 7547	**J** 7995
h 7247	**q** 7151	**A** 7640	
i 7797	**r** 7137	**B** *black*	
	s 7726	**C** 7861	

FRESH FLOWERS

Transform an old chair by stitching a new needle-point cover, decorated with a colorful bouquet of flowers, and turn an eyesore into an elegant conversation piece: the idea is scarcely new, but the reason for its perennial success is that it works so well and so beautifully. The background in this case is given interest by a simple geometric design and in order to vary the effect the French artist used a larger scale of canvas for the seat than for the back and sides of the chair, changing the size of the pattern.

Size Adjustable to fit any chair; the flower bouquet measures approximately 10in (25cm) from top to bottom and 8in (20cm) across.

MATERIALS

Single-thread 16-gauge canvas for the back and side panels
Single-thread 14-gauge canvas for the seat cushion
Tapestry needles size 20 and 18
Rotating embroidery frame or

wooden stretchers large enough to accommodate each piece of canvas
Fine-tip waterproof felt marker
Medium-tip felt marker

Note Chairs differ greatly in shape and design, and unless you have advanced upholstery skills you will probably choose to have your chair reupholstered professionally, so we have not explained how to fit the cover. Take all measurements very carefully (if possible, remove the old upholstery and measure this flat), making generous allowance for tuck-ins and seam allowances.

Threads

For the bouquet, *DMC tapestry wools:* one skein each of **red** *7107, 7606 and 7946,* **orange** *7439,* **mauve** *7120,* **violet** *7243, 7251, 7255 and 7709,* **peach** *7917,* **pink** *7133, 7204, 7260, 7600, 7603 and* *7804,* **blue** *7304, 7313, 7314, 7317 and 7800,* **green** *7327, 7369, 7384, 7386 7420, 7424, 7549, 7583, 7771, 7912 and 7956,* **yellow** *7433, 7681 and 7725,* **beige** *7423 and 7579,* **cream** *7745,* **ecru** *and* **white***.*

For the back, side panels, cushion cover and bouquet background the following colors of DMC tapestry wool are used: green 7369, 7386, 7420 and 7424.

Embroidery stitches

Half cross stitch, slanting satin stitch and straight stitch.

Note
To calculate the amount of thread needed for your chair, embroider a 4in (10cm) square of the pattern to use as a guide, stitching as follows: main color 7424, second color 7369, third color 7386 and fourth color 7420.

DIRECTIONS

▦ Measure each section of the chair widthwise and lengthwise. Draw the outline of each section on the appropriate canvas, bearing in mind that the finished pieces of embroidery should be approximately ⅜in (1cm) larger than these measurements to allow for turnings. Allow at least 4in (10cm) of surplus canvas around each piece for mounting in the embroidery frame, for blocking, and for the upholstery.
▦ Trace the bouquet design for the back of the chair and enlarge it to the required dimensions (see page 6). Strengthen the design lines with the medium felt marker.
▦ Place the canvas for the back panel over the design, centering the bouquet inside the drawn outline. The design lines will now be visible through the canvas.

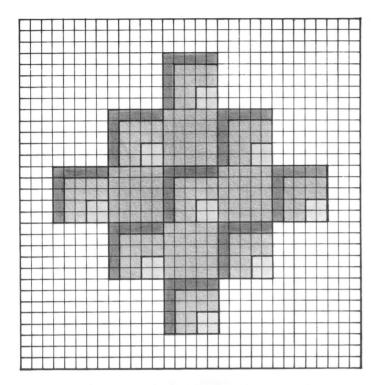

Using the waterproof felt marker, trace the design carefully onto the canvas.

▦ Mount the canvas in the embroidery frame or stretcher and begin the embroidery by working the flowers in irregular straight stitch. Work with the tapestry wool divided in half in the smaller needle and use the photograph as a color blending and stitch guide. When all the flowers have been completed, fill in the background between them in half cross stitch, using the green thread 7424.

▦ Work the geometric pattern around the central motif in slanting satin stitch and half cross stitch. Follow the chart carefully and again work with the tapestry wool divided in half.

▦ Work the geometric pattern on the two side panels in the same way.

▦ Embroider the geometric pattern for the cushion sections on the coarser canvas, using the tapestry wool undivided in the larger needle.

▦ When all the embroidery has been completed block the sections (see page 6) if they have pulled out of shape, paying special attention to the geometric pattern, which should be perfectly regular.

KEY

1	*7107*
2	*7439*
3	*7606*
4	*7946*
5	*7600*
6	*7603*
7	*7804*
8	*7133*
9	*7204*
10	*7260*
11	*7255*
12	*7709*
13	*7251*
14	*7120*
15	*7243*
16	*7917*
17	*7433*
18	*7725*
19	*7681*
20	*7745*
21	*7579*
22	*7423*
23	*ecru*
24	*white*
25	*7369*
26	*7384*
27	*7386*
28	*7420*
29	*7424*
30	*7549*
31	*7583*
32	*7771*
33	*7327*
34	*7912*
35	*7956*
36	*7304*
37	*7313*
38	*7314*
39	*7317*
40	*7800*

Enlarge 1½ times

EASTER TABLECLOTH

Breakfast on Easter morning is a family ritual in France as elsewhere, complete with brightly colored eggs, Easter bunnies, lambs and all the other images of springtime and renewal. Here is a tablecloth in the full Easter tradition, dotted with bells, flowers, rabbits seriously engaged in transporting their loads of eggs and hens apparently unperturbed by their multicolored produce. Children will enjoy it openly and adults secretly, and you will inevitably find yourself using it not just for Easter day but for birthday parties and a host of special occasions. These cheerful little designs are immensely versatile and could be used to decorate many other items for children, including pillowcases, pyjamas, T-shirts, bags, or even the hem of a nursery curtain.

Size 49½in × 49½in (124cm × 124cm).

MATERIALS

52in × 52in (130cm × 130cm) of fine white cotton fabric	Yellow and white sewing threads
4¾yd (4.2m) of ⅜in (1cm) wide yellow ribbon	Crewel needle size 5 or 6
	Dressmakers' carbon paper
	Large embroidery hoop

Threads
DMC stranded cotton: one skein of **yellow** 742 for the chicks; one skein of **blue** 995 for the ribbons; one skein of **brown** 921 for the rabbits; odds and ends stranded cotton in various shades of **green, blue, orange, yellow, beige, ecru, red, pink, mauve, gray, brown** and **black**.

Embroidery stitches
Satin stitch, long and short stitch, straight stitch, back stitch and stem stitch.

DIRECTIONS

▦ The two motifs shown above and those on page 26 are all shown full size. All other motifs are shown two-thirds full size.

▦ Trace all motifs, then take the small size ones and enlarge them to full size as described on page 6 (in this case the small grid should have ⅜in/1cm squares and the full-size grid should have ⅝in/1.5in squares). It may be easier simply to trace over the main outlines of the more complicated motifs and fill in the minor details by hand afterwards. Using the photograph as a guide to position, transfer the motifs to the fabric by the carbon paper method.

▦ Work with the fabric stretched in the embroidery hoop and re-position it as necessary. Embroider the motifs mainly in satin stitch and long and short stitch, picking out the details in stem stitch, back stitch and straight stitch. Use the close-up photographs as stitch and color blending guides and work with three strands of thread throughout.

▦ When the embroidery is completed, place the fabric face down on a well-padded surface and press it lightly, taking care not to crush the stitches.

FINISHING

▦ Turn under a double ⅝in (1.5cm) hem along all edges of the fabric, mitering the corners (see page 7). Pin and hem by hand.

▦ Cut the ribbon into four strips of equal length. Join the strips into a square, placing them right sides together and stitching the ends at a 45 degree angle to make mitered corners. Trim and press. Pin the ribbon square in place on the tablecloth, making sure that it is positioned an equal distance from the edge on all sides.

▦ Sew the ribbon to the tablecloth by machine, using either close zigzag stitches or a small running stitches, and keeping close to each edge of the ribbon. Stitch each edge in the same direction, to avoid ruckles.

VENETIAN ELEGANCE

Luxuriously elegant cushion covers and a table centerpiece to match make a light-hearted tribute to the great Italian architect of the sixteenth century, Andrea Palladio, who described the classical colonnades which often extended from his villas as 'arms to receive those who come near the house'. These sophisticated embroideries with their gentle, muted tones would blend perfectly with a neutral, modern setting, or with rag-rubbed or marbled walls.

Sizes The cushion covers measure 18½in × 18½in (47cm × 47cm); centerpiece 20in × 20in (50cm × 50cm).

MATERIALS

FOR EACH CUSHION COVER

16in × 16in (40cm × 40cm) of white linen or cotton fabric
Two 20in × 20in (50cm × 50cm) squares of dark fawn linen or cotton fabric
Matching sewing thread

Crewel needle size 5 or 6
Dressmakers' carbon paper in a dark color
Ruler and chalk marking pencil
Large embroidery hoop

CENTERPIECE

20¾in × 20¾in (52cm × 52cm) of white linen or cotton fabric
Matching sewing thread

Crewel needle size 5 or 6
Dressmakers' carbon paper
Large embroidery hoop

Threads

VILLA CAPRA ROTONDA

*DMC stranded cotton: one skein each of **shaded brown** 105, **brown** 433, **beige** 3046 and*
*3047, **gray** 535, 642 and 644, and **ecru***

VILLA GODI

*DMC stranded cotton: one skein each of **shaded brown** 105, **brown** 433, **gray** 415, 535*
*and 646, **blue gray** 927, and **ecru**, and two skeins of **gray** 3072*

VILLA PIOVENE

*DMC stranded cotton: one skein each of **shaded brown** 105, **brown** 407, **gray** 535, **peach***
*950, and **ecru**, and two skeins of **peach** 948*

CENTERPIECE

*DMC stranded cotton: one skein each of **gray** 3072, **blue gray** 926, **blue** 930, **peach** 948,*
*beige 950, and **fawn** 3046; two skeins of **fawn** 3047, and four skeins of **dark gray** 535*

Embroidery stitches

CUSHION COVERS

Satin stitch for the solid areas and back stitch for the lettering and borders.

CENTERPIECE

Satin stitch and cross stitch for the solid areas and back stitch for the outlines and lettering.

A

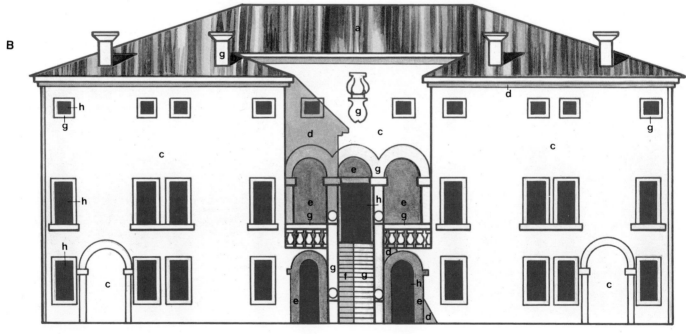

B

KEY
A
- **a** 105
- **b** 433
- **c** 3047
- **d** 3046

- **e** 642
- **f** 644
- **g** ecru
- **h** 535 *also* **B** *and* **C**

B
- **a** 105

- **b** 433
- **c** 3072
- **d** 927
- **e** 646
- **f** 415
- **g** ecru

C
- **a** 105
- **b** 948
- **c** 950
- **d** 407
- **e** ecru

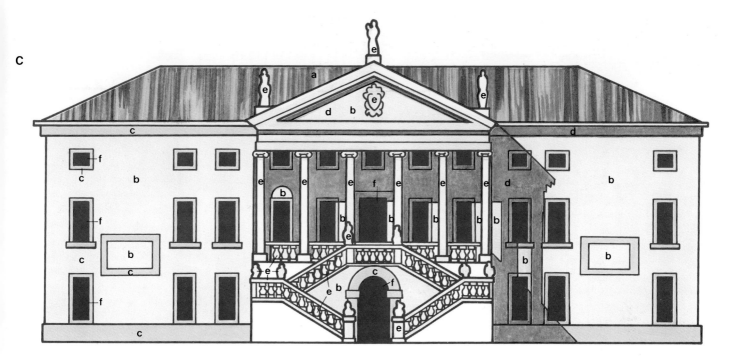

DIRECTIONS

CUSHION COVER

▦ Each cushion cover is made in the same way. Start by tracing the chosen design and enlarging it to the required dimensions, as shown on page 6.

▦ Transfer the design to the center of the white fabric using dressmakers' carbon paper. Draw in the border with the chalk pencil and ruler, approximately 2in (5cm) in from the raw edges of the fabric, following the grainlines.

▦ Using the photograph and diagram as stitch guides, embroider the solid areas of the design in satin stitch. Work the border and the appropriate lettering in back stitch using the gray thread, 535. Work with the fabric stretched in the embroidery hoop and use three strands of thread throughout.

▦ When the embroidery is completed, place the fabric face down on a well-padded surface and press it lightly, taking care not to crush the stitches.

FINISHING THE COVER

▦ On one piece of fawn fabric, cut out a central opening measuring 14in (35cm) square to accommodate the embroidered square. Turn under ⅝in (1.5cm) to the wrong side all around the opening, taking care to snip into the corners so that the fabric will lie flat. Tack the turning in place.

▦ Position the fabric over the embroidery so that the embroidery shows evenly through the opening, then pin and tack the layers together. Machine stitch through the fabric neatly around the opening 2mm (⅛in) from edge.

▦ Pin the front and back pieces of the cushion cover together with right sides facing. Taking a ⅝in (1.5cm) seam allowance, machine stitch them together around the edge.

▦ Trim the corners, press the seam and turn the cover to the right side.

▦ Insert the cushion pad and slipstitch neatly along the opening to close the cover.

ANDREA PALLADIO 1508-1580
VILLA CAPRA ROTONDA
VILLA GODI VILLA PIOVENE
VILLA ROTONDA

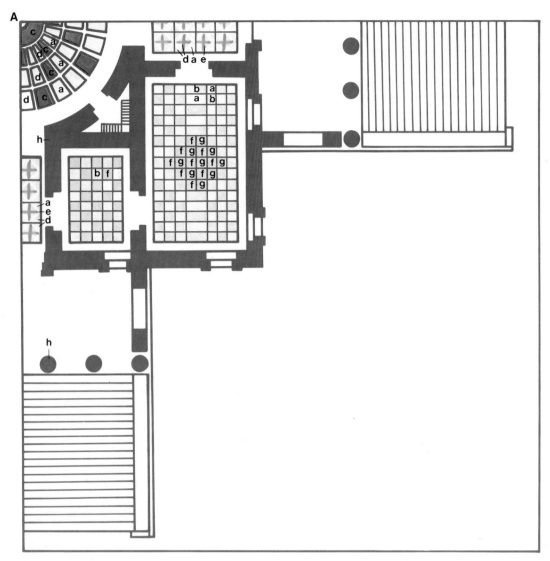

A

CENTERPIECE

▦ Start by making the border and finishing the edges of the cloth. Turn under and press a ⅜in (1cm) single hem all around the fabric square, mitering the corners neatly. Work a border of close machine zigzag stitch (or satin stitch by hand), covering the raw edges and making the hem.

▦ Between 3½in and 4in (6.5cm and 8cm) in from the edge of the cloth, make three narrow lines of satin stitch, set close together and running from edge to edge down each side, crossing at the corners.

THE EMBROIDERY

▦ One quarter of the design is shown, with A being the center point. Trace the complete design and enlarge it to the required dimensions following the instructions given on page 6.

▦ Transfer the design to the center of the cloth using the carbon paper method given on page 6.

▦ Using the photograph as a stitch guide, embroider the solid portions of the design in satin stitch and overstitch them with cross stitch where this is indicated on the design. Work the outlines and lettering in back stitch. Work with the fabric stretched in the embroidery hoop and use the three strands of thread throughout.

▦ When the embroidery is finished, place the cloth face down on a well-padded surface and press it lightly, taking care not to crush the stitches.

KEY

☐	**a**	*3047*
☐	**b**	*948*
■	**c**	*930*
☐	**d**	*3072*
▨	**e**	*926*
☐	**f**	*950*
▨	**g**	*3046*
▨	**h**	*535*

COUNTRY CONTENTMENT

Sit down to a refreshing cup of tea, secure in the knowledge that there is another cup in the pot, kept warm by a teacosy like a romantic rural idyll: a thatched cottage complete with leaded windows and rambling roses. The scale of this cottage would suit a small teapot. For a family-sized one you could add sky and clouds, finishing with blue cord instead of pink around the edge. The finished cover, with its warm interlining, is guaranteed to keep your tea hot while you daydream about a lazy summer in the country.

Size Approximately 7in × 11in (18cm × 28cm), to suit a small teapot.

MATERIALS

13in × 18in (33cm × 46cm) of double-thread 9-gauge canvas
Tapestry needle size 22
Fine-point waterproof felt marker
Rectangular embroidery frame or stretcher
1½yd (1.3m) of ¼in (6mm)

diameter pink cording (made or purchased, see page 39)
¼yd (30cm) of 36in (90cm) wide pink lining fabric
Beige and pink sewing threads
¼yd (30c,) of 36in (90cm) wide medium-weight polyester or cotton wadding

Threads

Anchor stranded cotton: two skeins each of **pink** 35 and 54, **beige** 372 and 376, **green** 842, 887 and 888, **brown** 357, 379 and 380, **gray** 393, **brick** 339,

yellow 302 and 311, **mauve** 104, **black** 403, and **white** 1, and four skeins each of **brown** 368, and **beige** 387

Embroidery stitches

Cross stitch and lattice stitch for the canvaswork and back stitch and herringbone for making up the cosy.

DIRECTIONS

▦ Using the felt marker, draw a line across the width of the canvas to divide it into two equal rectangles, one for the front of the teacosy and one for the back. Draw a vertical line through the center of each canvas rectangle, taking care not to cross any vertical threads. Mark the central horizontal line across each rectangle. Rule corresponding lines across the chart to find the center of the design.

▦ Mount the entire canvas in the embroidery frame or stretcher. On one canvas rectangle, embroider the cottage, starting at the center of the design and working outwards in cross stitch, following the chart square by square. Use

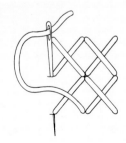

six strands of thread throughout. Work over the windows in lattice (large herringbone) stitch using the black thread.

▦ Embroider the cottage design again on the remaining canvas rectangle. When all the stitching is completed, block the canvas carefully, following the instructions given on page 6.

FINISHING

◫ Separate the two embroidered sections and trim away the unworked canvas from both pieces of embroidery, leaving a margin of ¾in (2cm) all around.

◫ Cut two pieces of lining to the same size and shape as the canvas (omitting the chimney tops), and two pieces of wadding ¾in (2cm) smaller all around.

◫ Place the two pieces of embroidery with right sides facing and, using beige thread, backstitch them neatly together, leaving the lower edge open. Turn under the lower edge right up to the embroidery and secure it with a row of herringbone stitch.

◫ Place one piece of wadding over one side of the embroidery, trimming it to the correct shape if necessary. Lay one piece of lining over the wadding and tuck the raw edges neatly between the wadding and the embroidery. Pin the layers in position and then slipstitch the lining neatly to the embroidery, using pink sewing thread. Repeat for the other side of the teacosy.

◫ Turn the teacosy to the right side and hand stitch the cording neatly around the edges as shown on the photograph.

MAKING CORDING

You can either use purchased cording or make your own, with lengths of pink perlé or crochet cotton. First twist strands together to decide how many strands you will need to make ¼in (6mm) diameter cording. To make 1½yd (1.3m) of cording, cut strands 4¾yd (4.1m) long. Put the strands together in one long bunch, with ends level. Tie the bunch in a knot at one end, and slip this end over a hook. Holding the other end of the bunch firmly, twist the strands tightly together. When the entire length is tightly twisted, place one finger at the center and bring the free ends level with the knotted ends. Remove your finger and the strands will twist into a cord. Trim

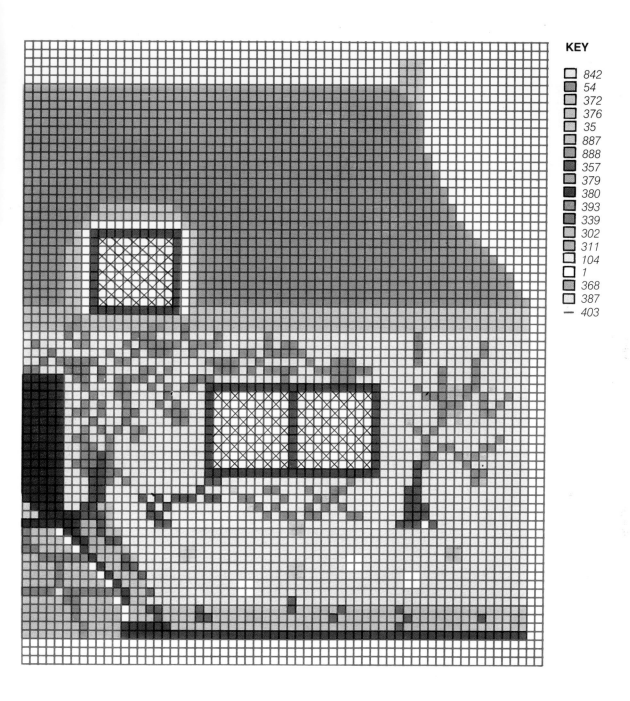

KEY
- 842
- 54
- 372
- 376
- 35
- 887
- 888
- 357
- 379
- 380
- 393
- 339
- 302
- 311
- 104
- 1
- 368
- 387
- — 403

away the first knot and knot all ends together. At the folded end of the cord, make another knot and trim the fold. If desired, use strands of different colors to produce multicolored cording.

HUNGARIAN DUVET COVER

Hungarian folk art captures the profusion and rich colors of tender wild flowers in vivid embroideries that hum with life like a gypsy dance. Here, a collection of the flower motifs that are traditionally used to decorate Magyar blouses are entwined to make a deeper inner border for a glowing duvet cover. The result is splendid, but the cover is not as complicated to embroider as it might appear: the stitches used are basically very simple and the lavish effect comes from the well-planned use of colors.

Size Finished cover measures 54in × 80in, to fit standard single bed duvet.

MATERIALS

4¾yd (4.2m) of 56in (140cm) wide white cotton sheeting fabric
White sewing thread
1yd (1m) of nylon snap tape

Dressmakers' carbon paper in a dark color
Crewel needle size 3 or 4
Large embroidery hoop

Threads

DMC pearl cotton No. 5: three skeins each of **pink** 335 and 818, **shaded pink** 48, **green** 581, 895 and 993, **shaded green** 92, 101 and 122, **white, shaded brown** 105, and **shaded turquoise** 91, and four skeins each of **red**

666 and 814, **shaded red** 57, 99, 107 and 115, **orange** 900, 817 and 947, **shaded orange** 51, **yellow** 402, 973, and 977, **shaded yellow** 108 and 111, and **shaded blue** 67, 93 and 121

Embroidery stitches

Satin stitch and stem stitch

DIRECTIONS

THE EMBROIDERY

▨ First cut the fabric into two equal rectangles and set one aside for the back of the cover.

▨ Trace the three sections of the garland design and join them carefully into one continuous strip. Enlarge the design to the required dimensions, as shown on page 6, again using tracing paper so that you can reverse it.

▨ Using the diagram as a guide to position, transfer the garland sections to the fabric.

▨ Working with the fabric stretched in the embroidery hoop, embroider the flowers and foliage in satin stitch and the stems in stem stitch.

▨ When the embroidery is completed, place the fabric face down on a well-padded surface and press it lightly, taking care not to crush the stitches.

FINISHING THE COVER

▨ Fold under and stitch a double 1in (2.5cm) hem along the bottom edge of front and back pieces.

▨ Place the front and back together, with right sides facing, aligning the hemmed edges. Sewing along the hemline, machine stitch the two pieces together for 10in (25cm) from each side, leaving a central opening.

▨ Trim the snap tape to measure 1¼in (3cm) longer than the opening. Position the two strips of tape along the edges of the opening so that they will match when the cover is turned to the right side. Stitch along the top and bottom edges of each strip, sewing through the hemmed edge only. Stitch the hems together at each side of the opening, enclosing the raw ends of the tape.

▨ Fold the cover with wrong sides facing and make a French seam around the remaining three sides: pin and stitch ⅜in (1cm) from the edge along all three sides and trim back to ¼in (6mm). Turn the cover wrong side out and stitch along all three sides again, ⅜in (1cm) from the edge, enclosing the raw edges and completing the seam.

▨ Turn the finished cover to the right side and press the seams.

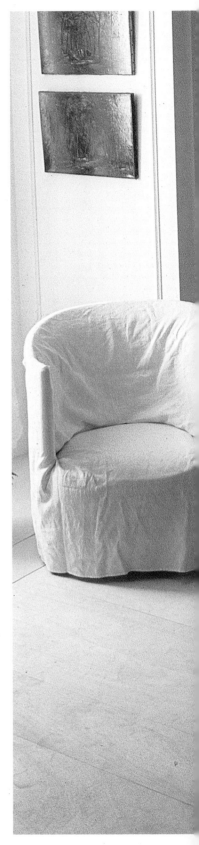

1 *Enlarge to make joined garland 20½in (74cm)*

2

It will help you to transfer the design if you first rule a base line on the fabric, using tailor's chalk. The line should be 29½in (74cm) long and positioned 24in (60cm) up from the bottom edge of the fabric, and an equal distance in from the sides. Using a set square, rule lines running upwards from each end of the base line, to act as guidelines for the side edges of the garland. The garland runs from **A** (left) to **B** (right) along the bottom line. The sides start with **C** at the bottom left and **A** at the bottom right, and finish with **B** at the top. The tracing is then turned over and repeated at the top, wrong side uppermost, to run from **B** at the top left to **A** at the top right, flower **A** being repeated at the top left to fill the gap between the two pattern repeats. When stitching the design, blend the colors to achieve a natural effect, varying them as indicated. For the flowers marked **1, 2, 3, 4, 5, 7** and **8**, use colors 115, 48, 57, 335, 107, 666, 818, 814, 900 and 99; flowers marked **6** and **10** are embroidered in colors 973, 977, 108, 402, 111, 817, 947, 51 and 105, and flowers marked **2** and **5** can also be stitched in these colors; for **11** and **12** use 67, 91, 93, 121 and white; and for **9** (stalks and leaves) use 92, 101, 122, 581, 895 and 993.

TROPICAL PARADISE

Size 56in × 56in (144cm × 144cm).

MATERIALS

1⅝yd × 1⅝yd (1.5m × 1.5m) of black cotton or cotton/linen fabric (the motifs are placed at random, so it does not matter if you choose to change the dimensions slightly)

Black sewing thread
Crewel needle size 3 or 4
Dressmakers' carbon paper in a light color
Large embroidery hoop

Threads

DMC Soft Embroidery Cotton: one skein each of **yellow** 2741 and 2743, **blue** 2597, 2599, 2797, 2798 and 2807, **gray** 2415, **green** 2347, 2595, 2788, 2952, 2954, 2956, 2957, 2905 and 2909, **orange** 2740, 2742, 2946 and 2947, **pink** 2351 and 2892, **red** 2349, **violet** 2209, **brown** 2299 and 2839, and two skeins each of **yellow** 2307 and 2745, **blue** 2826, and **gray** 2318

Embroidery stitches

Encroaching satin stitch, straight stitch, stem stitch and Chinese knots.

13

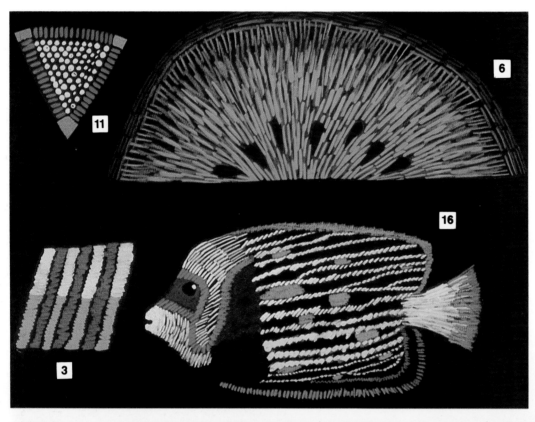

DIRECTIONS

▦ Trace the outlines of the motifs, all of which are shown half size, and enlarge them to the required dimensions, as shown on page 6. You will probably find it easier to fill in the minor details by hand, or to 'paint' them directly with your needle.

▦ Using the photograph as a general guide to position, transfer the outlines to the fabric, using dressmakers' carbon paper.

▦ Work with the fabric stretched in the embroidery hoop and re-position it as necessary. Embroider the motifs, using the photographs as stitch and color guides.

▦ When the embroidery is completed, place the fabric face down on a well-padded surface and press it lightly, taking care not to crush the stitches.

▦ Turn under a double ⅝in (1.5cm) hem along each edge of the square of fabric, mitering the corners, and hem by hand. Press the hem.

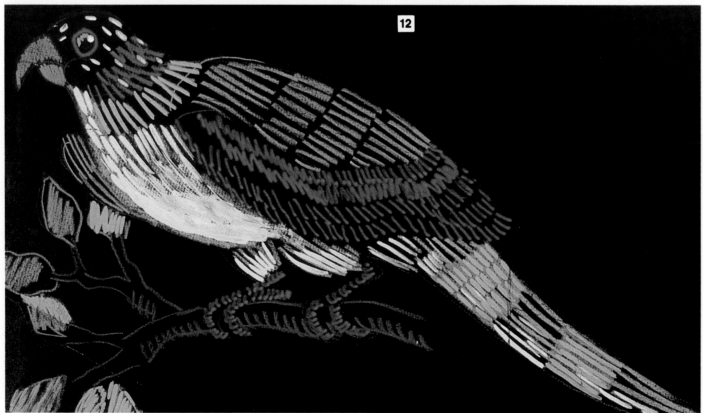

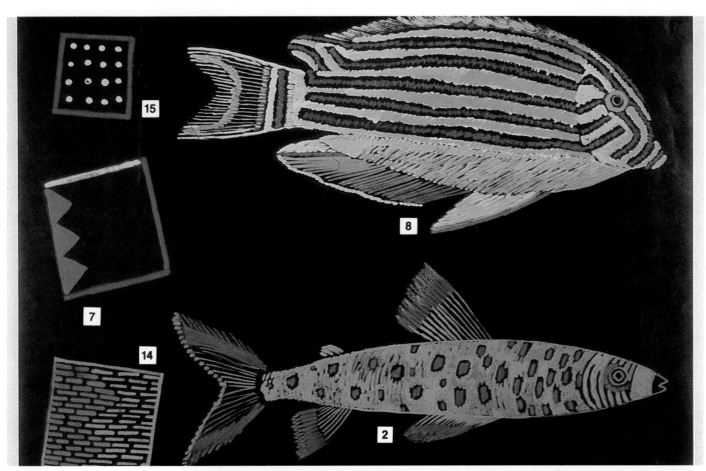

Colours used for each motif
1 2307 and 2956
2 2318, 2946 and 2347
3 2743, 2741 and 2826
4 2798 and 2957
5 2743, 2954 and 2351
6 2892, 2351, 2595, 2952 and 2954
7 2349 and 2892
8 2742, 2741, 2743, 2788, 2826, 2318 and 2415
9 2957, 2349 and 2798
10 2788, 2947, 2740 and 2742
11 2307, 2826, 2318, 2349 and 2209
12 2307, 2745, 2599, 2597, 2797, 2957, 2349, 2299 and 2839
13 2956, 2905 and 2909
14 2798 and 2318
15 2946 and 2307
16 2307, 2745, 2798, 2807, 2415 and 2299

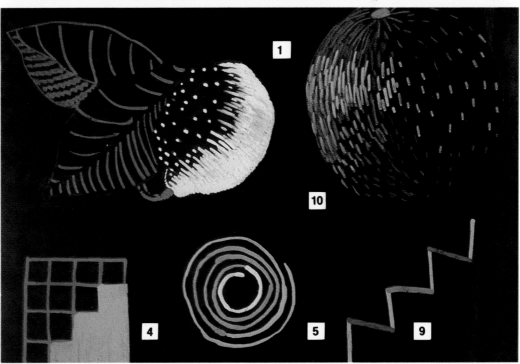

CULINARY ALLUSIONS

Whether your cuisine is enriched with fresh herbs snipped from your garden or a savory mixture of seafoods, these attractive aprons should help to make cooking a pleasure rather than a chore. The marine collection is embroidered entirely in stem stitch against a blue background, while the chives and parsley, complete with realistic-looking scissors and string, are embroidered in a variety of stitches. Both aprons are made to the same basic pattern, though the herbal version has patch pockets.

Size 32in × 32in (80cm × 80cm).

MATERIALS

SEAFOOD APRON
1yd (1m) of 36in (90cm) wide blue cotton fabric
Matching sewing thread
3yd (2.9m) of ¾in (2cm) wide matching blue tape

Dressmakers' pattern paper
Dressmakers' carbon paper in a light color
Crewel needle size 3 or 4
Large embroidery hoop

HERB APRON
1¼yd (1.1m) of 36in (90cm) wide white cotton fabric
Matching sewing thread
3yd (2.9m) of ¾in (2cm) wide white tape
Dressmakers' pattern paper

Dressmakers' carbon paper
Dressmakers' chalk pencil
Crewel needles size 6 and 7
Large chenille needle
Large embroidery hoop

Threads
SEAFOOD APRON
DMC stranded cotton: four skeins of **white**

HERB APRON
DMC stranded cotton: one skein each of **ecru, beige** 640 and 3047, **gray** 318, 414, 415 and 762, and two skeins each of **green** 122 and 988

Embroidery stitches
SEAFOOD APRON
Stem stitch

HERB APRON
Stem stitch, straight stitch, long and short stitch and Chinese knots.

DIRECTIONS

MAKING THE APRON
▦ Scale up the diagram on dressmakers' pattern paper and cut out. For the seafood apron, cut out the main piece and a matching pair of facings; for the herb apron, cut out the main piece, a pair of facings and two patch pockets.
▦ Taking a ⅜in (1cm) seam allowance and with right sides together, stitch a facing to each side of the apron, from neck edge to side edge. Holding facings out flat, make a narrow hem on all other edges, including short edges of facings. Turn under and press a ⅜in (1cm) seam along remaining long edge of each facing. Bring the facings to the underside of the apron and press.

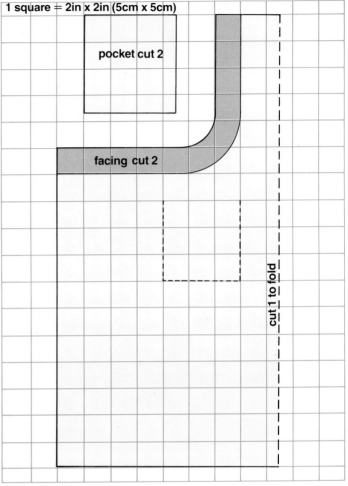

1 square = 2in x 2in (5cm x 5cm)

pocket cut 2

facing cut 2

cut 1 to fold

▦ Topstitch facings to apron, close to both pressed edges, leaving a casing for the tape.

▦ Cut the tape into two equal lengths and thread through the casing. Adjust to leave an adequate length for ties at neck and back, then stitch across at neck edge and side to hold ties in position.

▦ For herb apron, turn under ⅜in (1cm) and then 1in (2.5cm) along the top edge of each pocket section and stitch. Press under a double hem of ⅜in (1cm) on all other sides of each pocket and topstitch in place on apron.

SEAFOOD EMBROIDERY

▦ Trace the fish and shell design and enlarge it to the dimensions given, as shown on page 6.

▦ Following the photograph as a guide to position, transfer the individual motifs to the apron, using dressmakers' carbon paper.

▦ Working with the apron stretched in an embroidery hoop, embroider the motifs in stem stitch, using the stranded cotton double in the needle.

▦ When the embroidery is finished, place the apron face down on a well-padded surface and press it lightly, taking care not to crush the stitches.

HERB EMBROIDERY

▦ Scale up the chive and parsley motifs and, using the photograph as a guide to position, transfer them to the apron with dressmakers' carbon paper.

▦ Slip a pair of scissors into the other pocket and draw around the outline of the handles, using the dressmakers' chalk pencil. On the front of the same pocket, draw a line to represent the piece of string.

▦ Working with the apron stretched in an embroidery hoop, embroider the motifs as follows: the chives and parsley stems are worked in stem stitch, using two strands of green and the size 7 crewel needle.

▦ The bobbles on the parsley are formed by Chinese knots worked with six strands of green 988 and 12 strands of green 122 together in the chenille needle. They are linked to the parsley stems with

1 square = 1in x 1in (2.5cm x 2.5cm)

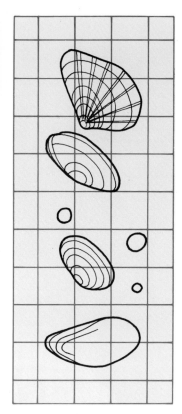

straight stitches, worked with two strands of the same green as the relevant stem and using the size 7 needle.

▦ Embroider the string in stem stitch, using six strands each of ecru, beige 640 and beige 3047 together in the chenille needle.

▦ The scissors are embroidered in long and short stitch in the four shades of gray. Use three strands of thread in the size 6 crewel needle and blend the colors from light to dark to achieve the effect of light shining at an angle on the scissors.

VARIATIONS IN GREEN

In some hot countries, the people weave leafy branches above their beds to create a cool atmosphere: this tender green design could have the same soothing effect. It features fronds of the castor-oil plant, copied from a botanical drawing and worked in a wide range of greens to create a realistic effect. The design here is shown on a large pillow of a type not generally found outside France, so the quantities and dimensions quoted have been adjusted to make a standard single duvet cover.

Size 54in × 80in (136cm × 200cm).

MATERIALS

7yd (6.3m) of 56in (140cm) wide white fabric with an even weave 1yd (1m) of nylon snap tape White sewing thread	Dressmakers' carbon paper in a dark color Crewel needle size 3 or 4 Large embroidery hoop

Threads

DMC pearl cotton No. 5: two skeins each of **gray** 644, 647 and 648; **green** 320, 367, 368, 369, 469, 470, 471, 472, 500, 503, 504, 703, 904, 911, 954,	966, 987 and 989, and (optional) two skeins of DMC stranded cotton in **white** (if you wish to make a drawn-threadwork hem)

Embroidery stitches
Straight stitch, running stitch, stem stitch, Chinese knots, back stitch and hem stitch (optional).

DIRECTIONS

▦ The designer used an old cover with a drawn-threadwork pattern and superimposed her own design over this. The drawn-threadwork hem stitching is not an essential part of the design, and it would be simpler to omit the lines running straight across the leaf design. If you decide to keep the lines of drawn-threadwork which border the design and edge the frill, make these before beginning the leaf embroidery.

▦ Cut the two main pieces, each measuring 56in × 83¾in (140cm × 209.5cm) from the fabric. Cut the remaining fabric into 8in (20cm) wide strips and join these to make a continuous strip for the frill. Turn under and press a double ⅜in (1cm) hem along one edge. If you are not working a decorative edge, stitch the hem of the frill in the standard way.

▦ If you are working the hem-stitched borders, make them at this stage along the hem of the frill and running parallel to the sides of the main fabric piece, 6in (15cm) in from the raw edges, using the photograph as a guide to position. Stitch the borders in the same way as the border of the napkin on page 62, catching in the hem along the frill and making a purely decorative border (no hem) around the main fabric piece.

▦ Trace the leaf design and enlarge it to the required dimensions, following the instructions given on page 6. Using dressmakers' carbon paper, transfer the design to the center of the fabric.

▦ Working with the fabric stretched in the embroidery hoop and using the photograph as a color and stitch guide, embroider the leaf design mainly in straight stitch and running stitch,

strengthening the outlines with back stitch and stem stitch. Use Chinese knots to pick out the details on the seeds.

▦ When the embroidery is finished, place the fabric face down on a well-padded surface and press it lightly, taking care not to crush the stitches.

FINISHING THE COVER

▦ Divide the frill into four equal

sections and mark with pins. Gather each frill section in turn.

▦ Mark the central point on the *seam line* at each edge of the front section of the cover. The seam line is 3in (7.5cm) in from the raw edge along the bottom and ¾in (2cm) in along the remaining three sides.

▦ Position the frill on the front, with right sides together and the finished edge of the frill lying inwards. The frill has a ⅝in (1.5cm)

seam allowance, so match seam lines, not raw edges.

▦ Matching marked points, pull up the gathering stitches of each section of the frill in turn. Pin and stitch the frill in place along the edges of the front.

▦ Trim the seam allowance on the frill only to ¼in (6mm). Finish the cover as described for the cover on page 40, making sure that the frill lies inwards.

KEY

a 966	**i** 989	**q** 503
b 504	**j** 904	**r** 500
c 369	**k** 471	**s** 648
d 368	**l** 470	**t** 644
e 320	**m** 469	**u** 647
f 367	**n** 911	
g 954	**o** 987	
h 472	**p** 703	

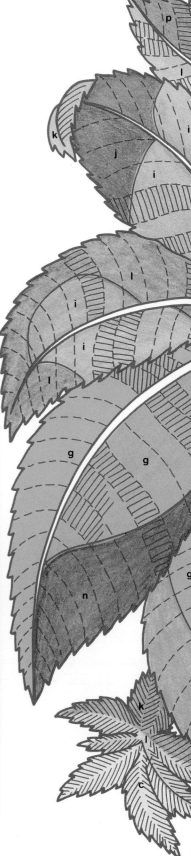

HOLIDAY SOUVENIRS

Practicality and beauty are combined in these two shopping bags, both of which are so pretty that they can be displayed on your kitchen wall when not in use. Alternatively, the designs could be used to make an attractive pair of cushion covers.

Size Each bag measures 15½in × 13in (39cm × 32.5cm).

MATERIALS

FOR ONE BAG

12in × 15in (24cm × 32cm) of single thread 12-gauge canvas
⅝yd (50cm) of 36in (90cm) wide strong linen or cotton fabric in a neutral color
Matching sewing thread

⅝yd (50cm) of 36in (90cm) wide lining fabric in a neutral color
Fine-point waterproof felt marker
Rectangular embroidery frame or stretcher
Tapestry needle size 20 or 22

Threads

SEASCAPE BAG

DMC soft embroidery cotton: one skein each of **brown** 2400 and 2829, **gray** 2413, 2414, 2647 and 2933, **black** 2310, **blue** 2595 and 2807, **green** 2502, 2504, 2715 and 2926, and **ochre** 2575 and 2738, and two skeins each of **white**, **gray** 2415 and **green** 2928

MOUNTAIN BAG

DMC soft embroidery cotton: one skein each of **green** 2856, 2926 and 2928, **brown** 2801, **gray** 2233, 2931 and 2933, **beige** 2302, 2543 and 2842, **yellow** 2745, **cream** 2579, **ochre** 2833, and **red** 2304 and 2918, and two skeins each of **white** and **gray** 2415

Embroidery stitches

Both designs are worked in half cross stitch, each square representing one half cross stitch.

DIRECTIONS

THE EMBROIDERY

▦ Both pictures are stitched in the same way: start by drawing a vertical line with the felt marker down the center of the canvas rectangle, taking care not to cross any vertical threads. Mark the central horizontal line in the same way. Rule corresponding lines across the appropriate chart to find the center of the design.

▦ Mount the canvas in the embroidery frame or stretcher. Begin stitching the design at the center and work outwards in half cross stitch, following the appropriate chart square by square.

▦ When all the stitching is complete, block the canvas carefully, as explained on page 6.

MAKING THE BAG

▦ Cut out two pieces measuring 16¾in × 14¼in (42cm × 35.5cm) from the main fabric and two pieces the same size from the lining fabric. From main fabric only, cut two strips measuring 3in × 16in (7.5cm × 40cm).

▦ Take one main fabric piece for the front of the bag and, using a pencil, mark out a window for the picture, making it 1¼in (3cm) smaller each way than the dimensions of the embroidered area. The window should be an equal distance from the side and bottom edges of the fabric, and

slightly closer to the top edge.

▦ Cut away the central portion of fabric and turn under an allowance of ⅝in (1.5cm) all around the opening, clipping into the corners so that the fabric will lie flat. Tack the turnings.

▦ Position the fabric over the embroidery and tack in place. Machine stitch around the opening, close to the folded edge.

▦ With right sides facing, pin bag front and back together and machine stitch them together along the sides and bottom edge, taking a ⅝in (1.5cm) seam allowance. Press the seam and turn the bag right side out. Stitch the lining sections together but do not turn them right side out.

▦ Fold each handle strip in half lengthwise, with right sides facing, and machine down the long side, taking a ⅜in (1cm) seam allowance. Turn right side out and press.

▦ Take one handle and position it on the front of the bag, with the raw ends of the handle matching the raw top edge of the bag. The ends should be in line with the side edges of the picture. Stitch across, taking a ⅝in (1.5cm) seam. Stitch the other handle to the back of the bag.

▦ Bringing the handles up, turn under ⅝in (1.5cm) around the top edge of the bag and press. Machine stitch around the three seamed edges of the bag, stitching close to the edge. Turn under and press the raw top edge of the bag lining. Slip it into the bag, then pin and stitch the bag and lining together, machine stitching close to the folded edges.

MOUNTAINEER BAG

KEY

■	2856
■	2926
■	2928
■	2801
■	2233
■	2931
■	2933
■	2302
■	2543
■	2842
■	2745
■	2579
■	2833
■	2304
■	2918
■	2415
□	white

SEASCAPE BAG

KEY

■	2400
■	2829
■	2413
■	2414
■	2933
■	2310
■	2595
■	2807
■	2502
■	2504
■	2715
■	2926
■	2575
■	2738
□	white
■	2647
■	2415
■	2928

CHARACTER NAPKIN

The ultimate refinement for a table set with traditional blue-and-white porcelain ware, this napkin decorated with drawn-threadwork and Chinese characters worked in padded satin stitch will add to the authenticity of any Chinese meal.

Size 16¾in × 16¾in (42cm × 42cm).

MATERIALS

18in × 18in (45cm × 45cm)
  square of fine white evenweave
  cotton or linen fabric
Crewel needle size 6 or 7

Dressmakers' carbon paper in a
  dark color
Embroidery hoop

Threads
DMC stranded cotton: one skein
  each of **blue** 798 and **white**

Embroidery stitches
Padded satin stitch for the motifs and hem stitch for the border.

DIRECTIONS

BORDER EMBROIDERY
▥ Withdraw sufficient threads to make a narrow border around the square of fabric, approximately 1in (2.5cm) from the raw edge. Finish the drawn corners by threading short lengths of the strands back into the fabric.
▥ Turn under ¼in (6mm) and then turn a hem so that the fold is just below the edge of the border. Miter the corners (page 6), and pin and tack the hem in place.
▥ Work a row of hem stitching to secure the hem using three strands of the white thread. Take each stitch around a group of three or four threads, depending on the weight of fabric being used. Repeat the hem stitching at the other side of the border to make a ladder pattern. Press the hem.

MOTIF EMBROIDERY
▥ Trace the Chinese character motifs. Using the photograph as a guide to position, transfer the motifs to the napkin using the carbon paper method described on page 6. Stretch the napkin in the embroidery hoop.
▥ Begin the embroidery by forming the padding for the satin stitch. Do this by filling the outlined shapes with close lines of back stitch, using two strands of thread in the needle. Work the back stitch down the length of the shapes, rather than across them.
▥ Finish the embroidery by working satin stitch across the lines of back stitch, using four strands of thread. When the embroidery is finished, place the napkin down on a well-padded surface and press it lightly, taking care not to crush the stitches.

hem stitch

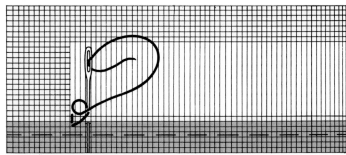

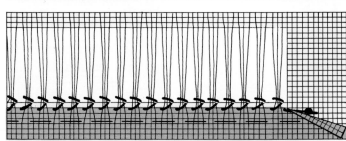

ladder pattern

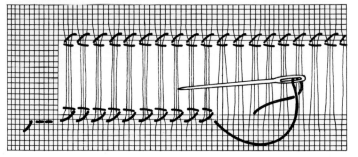

DAMASK DELIGHT

Sprays of pink and creamy flowers and grasses – unashamedly feminine and romantic – are set against a slightly unusual background of checkered pink damask, creating a feeling of elegance and great charm. The resulting tablecloth would look equally at home in a formal dining room, perhaps complemented by bowls of fresh flowers, or spread over a garden table. A matching cloth of striped pink and white cotton underneath protects the carefully embroidered damask and could be used to give it greater coverage.

Size 77½cm × 77½cm (194cm × 194cm).

MATERIALS

80cm × 80cm (200cm × 200cm) of pink and white checkered damask fabric Matching thread	Dressmakers' carbon paper Crewel needle size 4 or 5 Large embroidery hoop

Threads
DMC stranded cotton: one skein each of **gray** 415 and 452, **green** 368 and 3051, **pink** 335, 776, 778 and 819, and **blue gray** 927; two skeins each of **gray** 3024, **green** 3053, **pink** 223 and 3354, and **dull gold** 3032, and three skeins each of **green** 369, **gray** 642, and **beige** 822

Embroidery stitches
Long and short stitch, straight stitch, satin stitch, stem stitch and seed stitch.

DIRECTIONS

THE EMBROIDERY
▦ Trace the flower design and enlarge it to the required dimensions as shown on page 6. This is a complex design, and you may find that it helps if you number each square on both the smaller and larger grids when you are enlarging the pattern. Alternatively, you may prefer to concentrate on copying the main outlines accurately, filling in the smaller details by hand: your design may vary from the original, but only in minor respects.

▦ Using the photograph as a guide, transfer the motif to the corner of the fabric. Use the carbon paper method given on page 6 and position the design approximately 18in (45cm) in from the raw edges of the fabric.

▦ Working with the fabric stretched in the embroidery hoop, embroider the large flowers and areas of foliage in long and short stitch and the clusters of smaller flowers in satin stitch. Work the stems in stem stitch and the grasses in seed stitch and straight stitch.

▦ Use the photograph and the design as a guide when blending the colors, and work with four strands of thread for solid color areas and for shaded areas.

▦ When the embroidery is finished, place the fabric face down on a well-padded surface and press it lightly, taking care not to crush the stitches.

FINISHING
▦ Following a line of the checker pattern, turn a double ¾in (2cm) hem to the wrong side all around. Either make straight folds at the corners, or cut away spare fabric diagonally and make mitred folds.

▦ Pin and stitch the hem in place.

N/O A/N

B,E,C,D

To enlarge the design, first draw a grid on tracing paper, each square measuring ¼in × ¼in (5mm × 5mm). Trace over the main outlines of the design, then enlarge it onto a 1in (2.5cm) grid. Fill in any details by hand and transfer the design to the fabric. The letters show which colors are used in particular areas: where two letters are given together, for example H/K, use two strands of each color in the needle.

KEY

A 927
B 642
C 3024
D 822
E 369
F 368
G 776
H 223
J 335
K 3354
L 778

M 819
N 415
O 452
P 3051
R 3053
S 3032

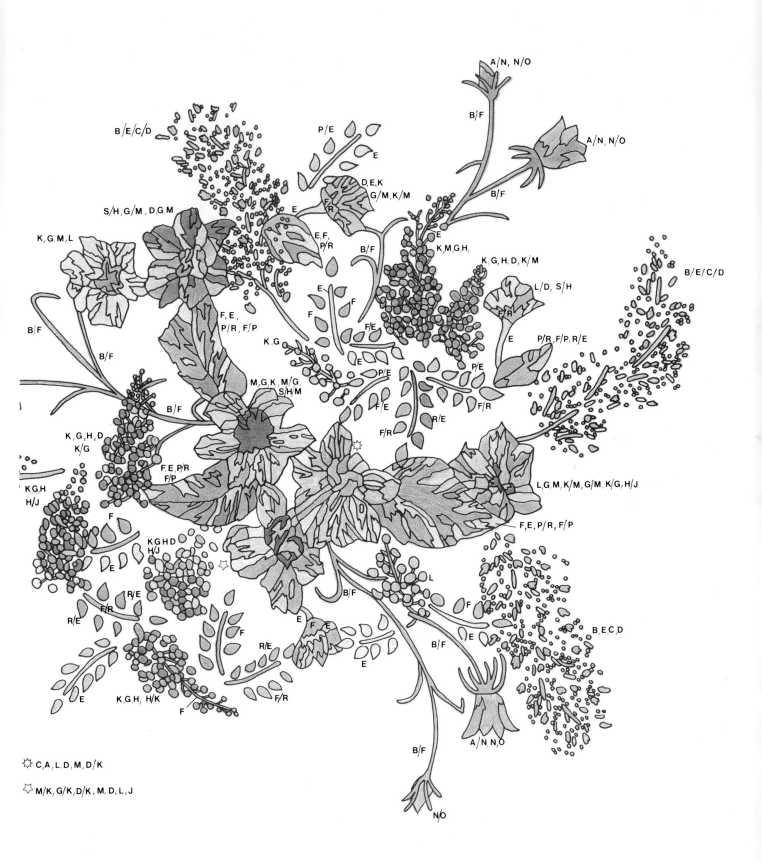

B/E/C/D

P/E

E

A/N, N/O

B/F

A/N, N/O

B/F

S/H, G/M, D,G,M

D,E,K
G/M,K/M

F/
R

K,G,M,L

E

E,F,
P/R

B/F

E

K,M,G,H,

K,G,H,D,K/M

B/E/C/D

B/F

F,E,
P/R,F/P

E

F

K,G

F

F/E

L/D, S/H

F/
R

E

P/R,F/P,R/E

B/F

M,G,K,M/G,
S/H/M

P/E

E

P/E

F/E

F/R

K,G,H,D
K/G

R/E

F,E,P/R
F/P

F/R

KGH
H/J

F

L,G,M,K/M,G/M,K/G,H/J

F,E,P/R,F/P

KGHD
H/J

E

L

R/E

B/F

F

R/E

B,E,C,D

F/R

E

F

F E

B/F

R/E

E

E

F/R

A/N, N,O

E

K,G,H, H/K

F

B/F

☆ C,A, L,D,M, D/K

☆ M/K, G/K, D/K, M, D, L, J

N/O

NATURE OBSERVED

Sunday in the country, French style, requires an elegantly packed picnic feast, complete with a freshly laundered tablecloth of enormous charm. The cloth is scattered with fruit, nuts, seed heads and insects, the latter so meticulously observed and so lifelike that they might just have jumped on to share the feast. Some 31 colors are used to create this gem of botanical accuracy, but the result is so delightful that it is well worth the attention to detail and the extra effort involved.

Size 77in × 91½in (192cm × 232cm).

MATERIALS

2⅝yd (2.4m) of 80in (200cm) wide fine cream linen or cotton fabric
Matching sewing thread

Dressmakers' carbon paper
Crewel needle size 6 or 7
Large embroidery hoop

Threads
DMC stranded cotton: one skein each of **brown** 435, 632, 898 and 3064, **green** 367, 471, 472, 734, 3051 and 3053, **yellow** 676, 726 and 3078, **blue** 826, **gold** 783 and 3045, **turquoise** 991, **rust** 918, **tan** 781, **beige** 822 and 3047, **cream** 712, **red** 350 and 498, **gray** 642, **white** and **black**.

Embroidery stitches
Satin stitch, long and short stitch and stem stitch.

DIRECTIONS

▦ Trace the motifs, which are shown full size.
▦ Using the photograph as a guide to position, transfer the motifs to the fabric with dressmakers' carbon paper.
▦ Work with the fabric stretched in the embroidery hoop, re-positioning it as necessary. Embroider the motifs mainly in satin stitch and long and short stitch, picking out the details in stem stitch. Use the close-up photograph as a stitch and color blending guide.
▦ Embroider the grasses, bee, small yellow insect and small blue insect using two strands of thread in the needle. Complete the rest of the design using three strands of thread throughout.
▦ When the embroidery is finished, place the fabric face down on a well-padded surface and press it lightly, taking care not

to crush the stitches.
▦ Turn under a double ¾in (2cm) hem all around the fabric and hem by hand. Press the hem.

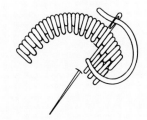

long and short stitch

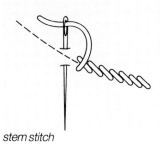

stem stitch

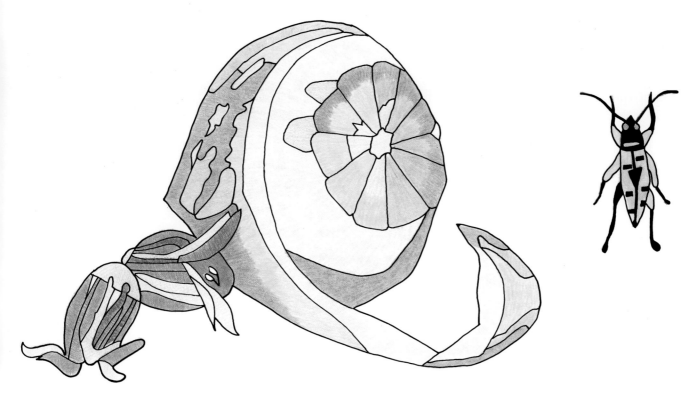

KEY

■	350
■	498
■	918
■	898
■	632
■	435
■	3064
■	781
■	783
□	726
■	676
□	3078
■	3047
■	3045
■	822
□	712
■	3051
■	367
■	471
□	472
■	3053
■	734
■	826
■	991
■	642
■	black
□	white

FALL OF LEAVES

A delicate shadow-work tablecloth of fine organdy, with napkins to match, captures the autumnal splendor of a French forest of sweet chestnut trees at that transitional time of year when the leaves begin to drift earthwards and the nuts ripen to form a delicious harvest to savor through the winter. In this embroidery technique, worked here with the traditional closed herringbone stitch, the threads are carried across the reverse side of a semi-transparent fabric. As shown below, the stitches can be worked from either side of the fabric, and they are used here to convey the impression of sunlight filtering through branches.

Size The tablecloth measures 42in × 77in (107cm × 192cm); each napkin measures 16in × 16in (40cm × 40cm).

MATERIALS

45in (115cm) wide fine cotton organdie as follows:	*Matching sewing thread*
2½yd (2m) for the cloth	*Crewel needle size 8 or 9*
17½in × 17½in (44cm × 44cm) for each napkin	*HB lead pencil*
	Large embroidery hoop

Threads
*DMC stranded cotton: one skein each of **brown** 355, 632, 780, **rust** 922 and 976, **gold** 729, and **green** 469, 470, 3051 and 3348*

Embroidery stitches
Closed herringbone stitch worked on the reverse of the fabric

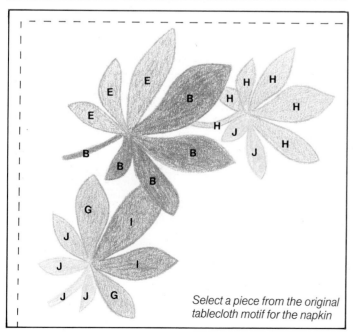

Select a piece from the original tablecloth motif for the napkin

DIRECTIONS

▣ Trace the leaf design and enlarge it to the required dimensions, as shown on page 6.

▣ Using the photograph as a guide to position, transfer the design to the fabric by placing the design under the fabric and tracing it through with the HB pencil. The pencil lines should be on the wrong side of the fabric.

▣ Work with the fabric stretched in the embroidery hoop and reposition it as necessary. With fine fabric of this type it is best to bind your embroidery hoop to help to prevent any possible damage. Take a length of bias binding tape and wrap it firmly round the inner ring of the hoop until all the wood is covered. Secure the ends with masking tape. As a further precaution, and to prevent the fabric from moving in the hoop, place a sheet of tissue paper over the fabric before fitting it in the hoop, then tear away the center, revealing the area to be embroidered.

▣ Embroider the leaves on the reverse side of the fabric in closed herringbone stitch, using two strands of thread in the needle throughout.

closed herringbone stitch right side

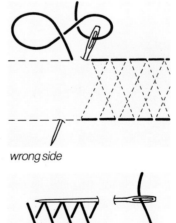

wrong side

⊞ When the embroidery is finished, place the fabric face down on a well-padded surface and press it lightly, taking care not to crush the stitches.

⊞ Turn under a double ¾in (2cm) hem all around the fabric and hem by hand or machine.

⊞ For the napkin, stitch the embroidery in the same way as for the cloth, but use the small leaf design. To finish the napkin, turn under a double ⅜in (1cm) hem and finish as for the cloth.

KEY

A	*355*
B	*632*
C	*780*
D	*922*
E	*976*
F	*729*
G	*469*
H	*470*
I	*3051*
J	*3348*

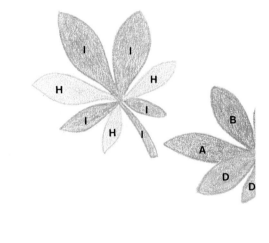

Enlarge 3 times

CHINA BLUE, POPPY RED

Blue-and-white porcelain vases are filled with the glorious tulips and poppies of late spring and early summer. Noone would pretend that these luxurious cushion covers are the sort of thing that you can complete in a day, but there is a great deal of pleasure to be gained from working with such a rich, lustrous and varied range of colors, and even more satisfaction to come, when your friends compliment you on the finished cushions.

chain stitch

Size Approximately 24in × 24in (60cm × 60cm).

MATERIALS

FOR ONE COVER
1½yd (1.4m) of 36in (90cm) wide closely woven white cotton fabric
Matching sewing thread
Crewel needle size 6 or 7

Large embroidery hoop
Tracing paper
Dressmakers' carbon paper
16in (40cm) zipper

Threads
FOR THE TULIP CUSHION
DMC stranded cotton: one skein each of **pink** *353, 604, 605, 776, 778, 818, 962, 3326 and 3684,* **yellow** *742, 743, 744, 972 and 973,* **flesh** *948,* **orange** *741,* **peach** *754,* **apricot** *352,* **white, ecru, gray beige** *644,* **wine** *814,* **green** *320, 368, 703, 987, 988 and 989,* **mauve** *316, and* **blue** *800, and three skeins of* **blue** *798*

FOR THE POPPY CUSHION
DMC stranded cotton: one skein each of **wine** *814, 3685 and 902,* **orange** *741 and 947,* **apricot** *350 and 351,* **blue** *800,* **yellow** *725 and 742,* **black** *310,* **green** *703, 704,* *904, 906, 907, 988 and 989,* **rust** *817, and* **pink** *353; two skeins each of* **red** *321 and 498,* **orange** *608, and* **apricot** *352; three skeins of* **blue** *798, and four skeins each of* **red** *606 and 666*

Embroidery stitches
TULIP CUSHION
Long and short stitch, satin stitch, stem stitch and chain stitch.

POPPY CUSHION
Long and short stitch, satin stitch, stem stitch and Chinese knots.

DIRECTIONS

TULIP CUSHION
▦ Cut a 28in × 28in (70cm × 70cm) square of cotton fabric. Cut two more pieces, each 25¼in × 13¼in (63cm × 33cm) and set these aside.
▦ Scale up the design on tracing paper and transfer it to the center of the fabric square, using dressmakers' carbon paper (see page 6).

▦ Work with the fabric stretched in an embroidery hoop, moving it as necessary. Three strands of thread are used throughout.
▦ Embroider the tulips and leaves in long and short stitch and the stems in satin stitch, using the chart as a color guide. No two people would reproduce this design exactly the same, stitch for stitch; the important thing is to embroider each petal separately, making sure that the color

changes blend gradually into each other, to give the effect of the subtle variations of tone to be found on flower petals.
▦ Work the vase mainly in satin stitch, picking out the details in stem stitch and the arabesques in chain stitch, using the photograph as a stitch guide.
▦ When the embroidery is complete, place it face down on a well-padded surface and press it lightly, taking care not to crush the stitches. Trim to measure 25¼in (63cm) square.
▦ Take the other two pieces of cotton fabric and place them right sides together. Pin and tack together down one long side, taking a ⅝in (1.5cm) seam allowance. At either side, stitch from the raw edge towards the center for 4⅝in (11.5cm), leaving a gap for the zipper. Insert zipper.
▦ With right sides together and zipper open, pin, tack and stitch cushion back to cushion front, around all the outside and taking a ⅝in (1.5cm) seam allowance. Turn right side out.

POPPY CUSHION
▦ Cut fabric, scale up and transfer design as for tulip cushion. Work with the fabric in an embroidery hoop, using three strands of cotton throughout.
▦ Embroider the flowers in long and short stitch and the stems in satin stitch, using the chart as a color guide. Pick out the poppy seeds in Chinese knots, using black thread. Work the vase mainly in satin stitch, with stem stitch for the linear details, using the photograph as a stitch guide.
▦ Press the finished embroidery and make up the cushion cover as for the tulip cushion.

KEY FOR TULIP CUSHION

a	353	q	352
b	604	r	white
c	605	s	ecru
d	776	t	644
e	778	u	814
f	818	v	320
g	3326	w	368
h	368	x	987
i	742	y	988
j	743	z	989
k	744	A	316
l	972	B	800
m	973	C	798
n	948	D	445
o	741	E	307
p	754	F	602

KEY FOR POPPY CUSHION

a	814	n	906
b	3685	o	817
c	741	p	321
d	947	q	608
e	350	r	352
f	351	s	353
g	800	t	798
h	725	u	606
i	742	v	666
j	310	w	743
k	703	x	922
l	704		
m	904		

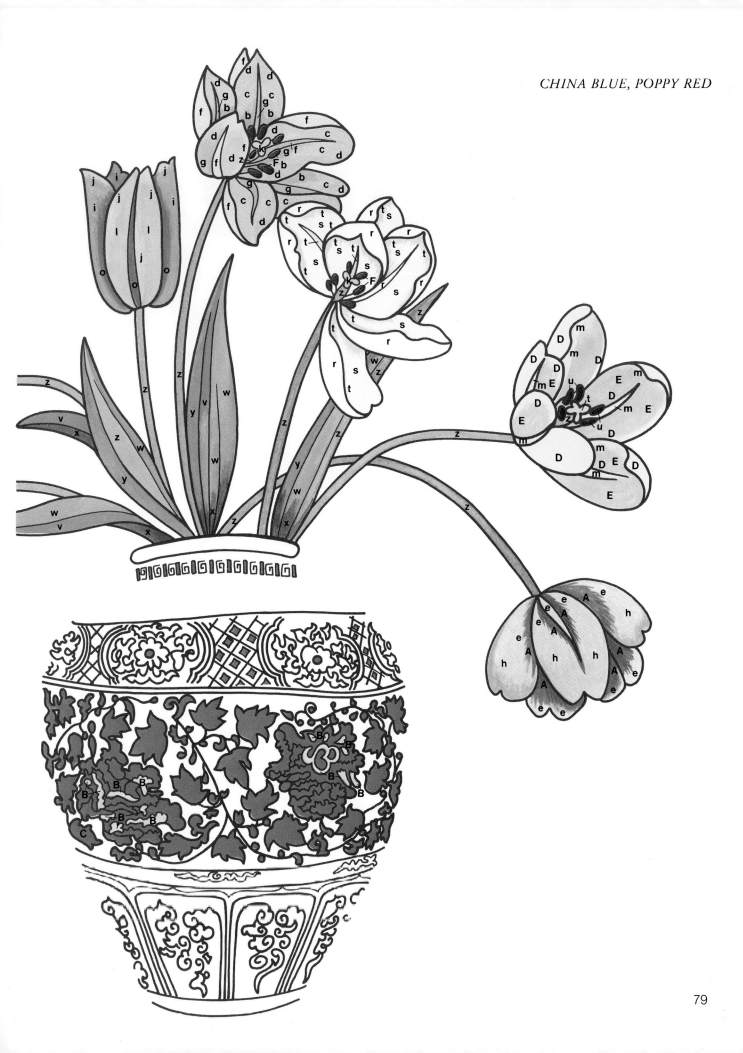